DoD 4140.50-R

DEPARTMENT OF DEFENSE

MANAGEMENT AND STANDARDS
OF
DOD
LOCOMOTIVES

JUNE 1985

ASSISTANT SECRETARY OF DEFENSE
(MANPOWER, INSTALLATIONS & LOGISTICS)

**MANPOWER,
INSTALLATIONS
AND LOGISTICS**

OFFICE OF THE ASSISTANT SECRETARY OF DEFENSE

WASHINGTON, D. C. 20301-4000

June 19, 1985

FOREWORD

This Regulation is issued under the authority of the Department of Defense (DoD) Instruction 4140.50, "Management of DoD Locomotives," December 9, 1982. Its purpose is to prescribe uniform procedures to execute the management policy set forth in DoDI 4140.50.

The provisions of this Regulation apply to the Office of the Secretary of Defense (OSD), the Military Departments, the Organization of the Joint Chiefs of Staff, and the Defense Agencies (hereafter called "DoD Components").

This Regulation is effective immediately and will be used by all DoD Components. Heads of DoD Components may issue supplementary instructions to provide more detailed guidance if required. Existing publications of the Department of the Army relating to the various phases of locomotive management may be used by other DoD Components in lieu of publishing their own instructions.

Send recommended changes to this Regulation to the Chairman, Interservice Locomotive Management Committee (Deputy Chief of Staff for Logistics, Headquarters, Department of the Army Attention: DALO-TSM).

DoD Components may obtain copies of this Regulation through their respective publications channels. Other federal agencies and the public may obtain copies from the Director, US Naval Publications and Forms Center, 5801 Tabor Avenue, Philadelphia, PA 19120.

Robert W. Daniel, Jr.
Deputy Assistant Secretary of Defense
(Logistics and Materiel Management)

TABLE OF CONTENTS

REFERENCES

(a) DoD Directive 5000.11, "Data Elements and Data Codes Standardization Program," December 7, 1964

(b) DoD 5000.12-M, "DoD Manual for Standard Data Elements," December 1982

(c) DoD Directive 5000.19, "Policies for the Management and Control of Information Requirements," March 12, 1976

(d) DoD Instruction 4140.50, "Management of DoD Locomotives," December 9, 1982

(e) DoD Instruction 4100.33, "Operation of Commercial and Industrial-Type Activities," February 25, 1980

(f) Federal Acquisition Regulation (FAR), current edition

C1. CHAPTER 1

GENERAL INFORMATION

C1.1. PURPOSE

C1.1.1. This Regulation establishes procedures to execute DoD Instruction 4140.50 (reference (d)). It designates a point of contact for DoD locomotive management information, a representative to chair the Interservice Locomotive Management Committee (ILMC), and the membership of the committee. It also establishes locomotive usage standards, locomotive replacement criteria, and procedures for maintaining current information on location, age, condition and usage of all locomotives in the Department of Defense.

C1.1.2. It establishes the duties of the Interservice Locomotive Management Committee and provides guidance on locomotive management, including authorization, selection of equipment, maintenance support, acquisition, and safety.

C1.1.3. The Regulation is designed to facilitate interservice support and coordination among the DoD Components in the management of DoD locomotives, and to establish a centralized inventory reporting system to readily identify locomotives available for assignment or reassignment to other Services.

C1.2. APPLICABILITY

The development and maintenance of this Regulation is authorized by DoD Instruction 4140.50, "Management of DoD Locomotives," reference (d). The Regulation applies to the Military Departments and the Defense Agencies (hereafter referred to as "the DoD Components").

C1.3. RESPONSIBILITIES

C1.3.1. The Secretary of the Army shall:

C1.3.1.1. Serve as the executive agent for the procurement of locomotives in the Department of Defense.

C1.3.1.2. Designate a point of contact for DoD locomotive management information.

C1.3.1.3. Pursuant to his responsibilities, establish and chair an Interservice Locomotive Management Committee, The Deputy Chief of Staff for Logistics, Headquarters, Department of the Army (HQDA), will provide a GM-13 representative to chair the Interservice Locomotive Management Committee.

C1.3.2. The <u>DoD point of contact</u> for locomotive management information shall:

C1.3.2.1. Maintain current DoD locomotive replacement criteria.

C1.3.2.2. Execute and maintain the Locomotive Management Information System specified in Chapter 3.

C1.3.2.3. Provide DoD Components, as requested, with current information on location, age, condition, and usage of locomotives in the Department of Defense.

C1.3.2.4. Provide a representative to serve as an ex officio member of the Interservice Locomotive Management Committee.

C1.3.3. <u>DoD Components</u> shall:

C1.3.3.1. Provide input for the Locomotive Management Information System to the DoD point of contact in accordance with Chapter 3.

C1.3.3.2. Advise DoD point of contact of its designated manager for locomotive management information and HQDA of its representative to the Interservice Locomotive Management Committee.

C1.4. <u>PROCEDURES</u>

This Regulation is tailored to provide policy guidance solely for locomotive management, although it is recognized that the operation of DoD rolling stock is often an intrinsic part of the locomotive management function. This Regulation may be augmented by the DoD Components to prescribe more detailed instructions, if necessary. Existing publications of the Army on the various phases of locomotive management may be used by the other DoD Components instead publishing their own regulations. Joint Service regulations are encouraged as an interim measure to ensure complete compliance with this Regulation. Matters requiring issuance of DoD policy, or amendment, or clarification of this Regulation should be referred to the chair of the ILMC. An objective of the ILMC is to consolidate, when possible, the DoD

Component publications into this Regulation to minimize the growing number of regulations, and ensure uniformity of policy and instructions.

C1.5. DEFINITIONS

C1.5.1. Motive Power. Railroad locomotives and other self-propelled equipment designed for moving rolling stock. This includes self-propelled rail cars designed to carry freight and/or passengers within the body of the car and car movers designed to operate interchangeably on either rubber tires or steel-flanged wheels.

C1.5.2. Rolling Stock. Railroad cars used for the movement of freight or passengers thath must be moved by a locomotive or other external means. Railroad cars are further categorized by their use or design as box, flat, depressed center flat, gondola, hopper, dump, tank, caboose, and passenger.

C1.5.3. Utility Railroad. Railroads that connect with rail carrier lines and range from a simple siding to a warehoue or series of warehouses to a complete rail network with interchange tracks, switching leads, repair tracks, inspection tracks, and any additional tracks necessary to facilitate the receipt and delivery of carload freight and provide a network for intra-installation transportation.

C1.6. REPORTING REQUIREMENTS

The Utilization Report specified in Chapter 3, section C3.5., is assigned Report Control Symbol DD-MIL(A)1683 in accordance with reference (c).

C2. CHAPTER 2

INTERSERVICE LOCOMOTIVE MANAGEMENT COMMITTEE (ILMC)

C2.1. OBJECTIVE

The primary objective of the Interservice Locomotive Management Committee (ILMC) is to conduct periodic reviews of locomotive management information and coordinate DoD Component locomotive replacement and distribution plans. A secondary objective of the ILMC is to facilitate an integrated management system for DoD locomotives through analysis of the locomotive management information and an interchange of expert advice. Regulations and policies of the DoD Components shall be reviewed and consolidated to the maximum extent and when feasible incorporated into this Regulation by amendment.

C2.2. REVIEW OF LOCOMOTIVE MANAGEMENT INFORMATION

A comprehensive review by each member of the ILMC shall be made of the locomotive management information furnished by their DoD Component. An analysis of the information shall be presented by each committee member at the annual meeting of the committee. The committee shall advise and assist the individual DoD Components in improving management techniques to achieve maximum usage of its assigned motive power; discussions shall be held on common management problems, and solutions will be sought that can be uniformly applicable within the Department of Defense. Information reporting procedures shall be reviewed annually to determine if revisions should be made to the Locomotive Management Information System (LMIS).

C2.3. LOCOMOTIVE REPLACEMENT AND DISTRIBUTION PLANS

The committee shall review the replacement and distribution plans of the locomotive managers of the DoD Components to determine if redistribution of excess or under-utilized locomotives is feasible. Loans of locomotive equipment to satisfy short-term or temporary requirements shall be considered. The use of Interservice Support Agreements (ISSAs) shall be encouraged by the ILMC to reduce the locomotive resource requirements within the Department of Defense.

C2.4. MEMBERSHIP OF THE INTERSERVICE LOCOMOTIVE MANAGEMENT COMMITTEE

Permanent members of the committee have been designated by the Heads of the DoD Components as indicated:

C2.4.1. Chair of ILMC. Designee of the Deputy Chief of Staff for Logistics, Headquarters, Department of the Army.

C2.4.2. Member. Designee of the Commander, Naval Facilities Engineering Command.

C2.4.3. Member. Designee of the Commander, Headquarters, Air Force Logistics Command.

C2.4.4. Member. Designee of the Commandant, Headquarters, U.S. Marine Corps.

C2.4.5. Member. Designee of the Director, Headquarters, Defense Logistics Agency.

C2.4.6. Ex Officio Member. To be designated by the DCSLOG, HQDA. The Chair may request the participation of technical or management experts in the meetings of the committee as required to accomplish the objectives of the ILMC.

C2.5. ILMC MEETINGS

The committee shall meet annually at time and place designated by the Chair. Additional meetings may be scheduled by the Chair as necessary to achieve the objectives of this Regulation.

C3. CHAPTER 3

LOCOMOTIVE MANAGEMENT INFORMATION SYSTEMS (LMIS)

C3.1. USAGE STANDARDS

The Heads of the DoD Components shall ensure that all installations within their respective Services that operate locomotives have a reporting system that can be effectively used to measure the utilization of the equipment. Due regard will be given to the mission of the installation, and the system may be tailored to reflect the peculiarities or constraints of certain installations. Existing systems for reporting utilization may be used if they contain the common measurable factors specified in the section C3.3., Locomotive Data File Layout, Columns 34 through 55. The utilization reporting system is to be based on transportation performance factors for rail operations. The common measurable standards are total switch movements, total rail cars switched, intra-plant car movements, inbound and outbound cars interchanged with the commercial carriers serving the installation, and similar operating data maintained in accordance with the DoD Components management and performance standards.

C3.2. INVENTORY

The Heads of the DoD Components shall designate a manager within their respective Services to maintain a master inventory record by locomotive type and location.

C3.3. RAIL DATA FILE LAYOUT

COLUMNS	DESCRIPTION
1-13	NSN
14-15	MFG YR
16-17	STATE
18-20	WEIGHT
21	MAJOR COMMAND
22	SERVICE
23	BLANK
24-29	LOC CODE (UIC)
30-33	INSP DATE
34-38	OPER HRS
39-42	ANNUAL GRS
43-46	CARS IN
47-50	CARS OUT
51-55	INTR SWITCHES
56	BLANK
57-71	ROAD NUMBER
72	CONDITION
73	REQUIREMENTS CODE
74-77	ACQUISITION COST

Data will be in:

1. 80 Column Card Form
2. Magnetic Tape, Autodin Record Length 80 Characters, BLKSIZE 3200 (40 Records/block)

C3.4. DESCRIPTION DEFINITIONS

NSN -- National Stock Number where known or established identification number.

MFG YR -- Calendar year locomotive manufactured or remanufactured in.

STATE -- State that installation and locomotive are located in.

WEIGHT -- Tonnage of locomotive.

MAJOR COMMAND -- Major Command to which installation is assigned.

D--DARCOM, F--FORSCOM, T--TRADOC, M--MTMC.

SERVICE - DoD Component -- A--Army, N--Navy, F--Air Force, M--Marine Corps, S--Defense
Logistics Agency.

LOC CODE - (UIC) -- Alpha-Numeric for each location.

INSP DATE -- Date of last technical inspection or date of reporting inventory: (Year/Julian date; i.e., 1 Jan 85 = 5001).

OPER HOURS -- Total accumulated hours since overhaul or remanufacture.

SEMI-ANNUAL HOURS -- Total hours locomotive operated last 12 months.

CARS IN -- Number of rail cars received (loaded or empty) by installation during past 12 months.

INTRA-SWITCHES -- Each rail car moved and spotted at a differnt location within an installation.

ROAD NUMBER -- Reporting marks and numbers identifying each locomotive.

CONDITION CODE -- A--Serviceable, F--Unserviceable, M--Being remanufactured or
overhauled -- or MIL-STRIP Condition Code.

REQUIREMENTS CODE -- 1 - In Use-Serviceable, 2 - Stand-by Serviceable,
3 - Contingency-Serviceable, 4 - Storage-Serviceable,
5 - Storage-Unserviceable, 6 - Excess-Serviceable,
7 - Excess-Unserviceable, 8 - Loan, 9 - In-Transit

ACQUISITION COST -- Cost in $000's.

C3.5. REPORTING PROCEDURE

C3.5.1. The usage report and locomotive inventory data required by sections C3.1. and C3.2. shall be submitted by the designated DoD Component managers on a annual basis to TROSCOM, the DoD point of contact for locomotive management information. The information will be transmitted in the rail data file layout specified in section C3.3. not later than 20 January each year.

C3.5.2. TROSCOM will produce a hardcopy database print, on request, and will provide each LMIC member a copy. Format for usage report hardcopy report is to be developed by TROSCOM.

C4. CHAPTER 4

MANAGEMENT OF LOCOMOTIVES

C4.1. GENERAL

Locomotives are characterized by a high initial acquisition cost, an extended procurement lead time, minimal technical obsolescense, and a long effective lifespan. These factors dictate a comprehensive analysis of locomotive requirements and a thorough review of all feasible alternatives to the ownership of this equipment. It is DoD policy to maintain and operate in peacetime a diversified fleet of motive power to provide for logistic needs and essential training of operational personnel to ensure military effectiveness in support of national defense policies. Locomotives shall be acquired and utilized with due regard to the availability of commercial transportation. Within the intent of this Regulation, the considerations to be given to the use of commercial transportation are outlined in section C4.2., below.

C4.2. COMMERCIAL CARRIER SWITCHING SERVICE

Rail Carrier Obligations: Line haul rates offered by carriers shall be deemed to include delivery to the unloading spot. Further, rail carriers may deliver on and remove cars from privately owned side tracks and industrial tracks connecting with a carrier's tracks, cars of freight moving at carload rates, without additional charge, provided there are no conditions that make it unsafe for the carrier's locomotives to operate over such tracks or that prevent carriers from receiving or delivering the cars at its <u>ordinary operating convenience</u> in a <u>continuous movement</u>.

C4.2.1. "Continuous movement" means a movement between the carrier's tracks and the loading or unloading locations, a hold track or tracks, or other place where cars are received or delivered without any delay, or any suspension, or break in time, or continuity of the movement, due to any circumstances or condition for which the industry is directly responsible.

C4.2.2. "Ordinary operating convenience" means the time selected by the carrier when it is most advantageous to the carrier, in relation to its coordinated switching activities in a particular switching zone, when the terminal services are performed by switching locomotives, or at the time the scheduled trains arrive at the plant site when the switching services are performed by road switcher. Ordinarily, it contemplates only one switch a day, except when additional switches are made for carrier convenience to secure the prompt release of equipment or when necessitated by the volume of traffic. Movements to, from, or within the plant site at other times, at the request of the industry are not considered at the carrier's ordinary operating convenience.

C4.2.3. Switching services required beyond the carrier's obligation for initial placement of a car, such as intra-plant switching and weighing operations performed by the installation for its own convenience, are transportation services that the carrier is normally not obliged to perform. However, these special switching services can be performed by carrier when agreed-to special charges are published. The installation Transportation Officer should request the rail carriers to establish special charges for these services if such agreements are not on file. The switching services of the rail carriers shall be used to the maximum extent possible. Shipping, receiving, and warehousing activities shall be scheduled and coordinated to gain full benefit of the carrier's services, augmented by the carrier's special contracts for respotting, intra-plant switches, weighing and similar services.

C4.2.4. Assistance may be requested through channels from the Commander, MTMC, if a satisfactory agreement cannot be reached with the concerned rail carriers.

CHAPTER 4

C5. CHAPTER 5

AUTHORIZATION OF LOCOMOTIVES

C5.1. POLICY

Prior to requesting the assignment of a DoD locomotive, the DoD Component initiating the request shall make an administrative determination that the installation requesting the locomotive has:

C5.1.1. Not been able to secure switching service on a tariff basis from the serving rail carrier or carriers.

C5.1.2. Complied with the provisions of OMB Circular No. A-76 and the implementing DoD Instruction 4100.33, "Operation of Commercial and Industrial-Type Activities," (reference (e)) and the associated DoD 4100.33-H, "DoD In-House Vs. Contract Commercial and Industrial Activities Cost Comparison Handbook.

C5.1.3. Determined it is not economically feasible to transfer the rail traffic to an alternate transportation mode.

C5.1.4. Determined it is necessary to meet mobilization requirement(s).

C5.2. REQUIREMENTS

Locomotive requirements shall be compatible with the organizational structure and mission of the installation.

C5.2.1. Locomotives shall be required on a continuing basis.

C5.2.2. There is no suitable substitute-type locomotive available at the installation.

C5.3. AUTHORIZATION

An authorization document shall be issued by the Head of the DoD Component or his designee specifying the type and quantity of locomotives to be assigned to the requesting installation.

C6. CHAPTER 6

SELECTION OF LOCOMOTIVES

C6.1. ANALYSIS OF REQUIREMENTS

The selection of a locomotive is based on the average daily switching requirements of the installation during both peacetime and mobilization. The majority of the DoD rail operations are utility railroad and intra-plant in nature, characterized by relatively short distance switch movements usually consisting of less than ten rail cars per move. Distances from the interchange points with the commercial rail carriers to the installation's classification or receiving yards rarely exceed five miles. Therefore, the criteria used by commercial rail carriers for the assignment of motive power are not generally applicable to the operation of a DoD installation. The daily average Gross Trailing Load (GTL) switching requirement of an installation should be used in computing the Drawbar pull (DBP) need for an assigned locomotive. During peak periods an extra switch move may be required to handle an above average volume of cars. This situation is preferable to the acquisition, assignment, use and maintenance of a locomotive larger than that required for the installation's mission. The objective is to assign locomotives of the minimum size and horsepower available that can effectively perform the switching requirements of the installation. Sections C6.2. and C6.3. contain formulas and factors to be used in the selection of a locomotive as well as characteristics of locomotives owned and operated by the DoD Components.

C6.2. FORMULAS AND FACTORS FOR LOCOMOTIVE SELECTION

Locomotives will be selected based upon consideration of the following factors.

C6.2.1. Weight on Drivers. Weight on drivers is expressed in short tons; it is that weight supported by the driving wheels of a locomotive. It does not include any of the remaining portion of the locomotive's weight. The weight on drivers of some locomotives used by the Department of Defense is shown in Table C6.T1.; for those not listed in this table, specifications issued by the purchaser, the using railroad, or the manufacturer must be consulted.

C6.2.2. Tractive Effort. The force developed at all the locomotive driving wheels parallel to the rail to move the locomotive and cars. This force is expressed in pounds; it is directly proportional to the locomotive horsepower and inversely proportional to the locomotive speed. The tractive effort of some locomotives used by the

Department of Defense is contained in Table C6.T1. Where such data are not available, tractive effort may be determined as indicated in subparagraphs C6.2.2.1. and C6.2.2.2., below.

C6.2.2.1. Starting Tractive Effort (TE).

C6.2.2.1.1. Starting tractive effort is the power that a locomotive can exert to move itself and the load that it is hauling from a dead stop. It is correlated closely to the adhesion that the driver wheels maintain at the rails. If the tractive effort expended exceeds this adhesion factor, the driving wheels will slip. Normally, the adhesion factor, when the rails are dry, is 30 percent of the weight on drivers; when the rails are wet, this factor is reduced to 20 percent. For planning purposes, 25 percent is used.

C6.2.2.1.2. For a diesel locomotive weighing 80 short tons (73 metric tons) or 160,000 pounds (72,574 kilograms) on the driving wheels, the starting tractive effort is computed as follows:

$$TE = \frac{\text{Weight on drivers (1lb(kg))}}{25\% \text{ adhesion factor}}$$

$$= \frac{160,000 \text{ lbs (72,574 kgs)}}{4}$$

$$= 40,000 \text{ lbs (18,143 kgs)}$$

C6.2.2.2. Continuous Tractive Effort TE. Continuous tractive effort is the effort required for the locomotive to keep a train rolling after it has been started. As the momentum of a train increases, the tractive effort necessary to keep the train moving diminishes rapidly. Since a diesel-electric locomotive cannot continue to exert the same force while pulling a load as was attained in starting that load, the continuous tractive effort of a diesel-electric locomotive is rated as approximately 50 percent of its starting tractive effort. For a diesel-electric locomotive weighing 80 short tons (73 metric tons) or 160,000 pounds (72,574 kilograins) on the driving wheels, the continuous tractive effort is computed as follows:

$$TE_c = \frac{TE}{2}$$

$$= \frac{\underline{40,000 \text{ lbs } (18,143 \text{ kgs})}}{2}$$

$$= 20,000 \text{ lbs } (9,071 \text{ kgs})$$

C6.2.3. Drawbar Pull (DBP)

C6.2.3.1. Drawbar pull is the force available to pull a train after deducting from tractive effort the energy required to move the locomotive itself. In planning, 20 pounds per ton of total locomotive weight is taken from the tractive effort as follows:

Total locomotive wt = 100 STON

100 x20 = 2,000 pounds

TE minus 2,000 pounds = DBP

or

TE = $\frac{2000,000}{4}$ = 50,000

TE = $\frac{50,000}{2}$ = 25,000

DPB = 25,000 - 2,000 = 23,000 pounds

C6.2.3.2. Maximum drawbar pull can be exerted only at lowest speeds up to about 10 miles (16 kilometers) an hour and for a limited length of time; at higher speeds, diesel-electric locomotive drawbar pull diminishes rapidly because the electric generator and traction motor cannot hold up under the heavy starting voltage and amperage, and would burn out if the load continued for a longer time after the locomotive reached a speed of 10 miles per hour. However, a steam locomotive retains its initial drawbar pull at all speeds in the same manner that it retains its tractive effort at all speeds.

C6.2.4. Rolling Resistance (RR). The force components acting on a train in a direction parallel with the track, which tend to hold or retard the train's movement, constitute rolling resistance. The components of rolling resistance are friction between the railheads and the treads and flanges on the wheels, resistance due to undulation of track under a moving train, internal friction of rolling stock, and resistance in still air. There is no absolute figure to be used for rolling resistance, but experience indicates that safe average values to use for rolling resistance are as shown in table C6.T2.

C6.2.5. <u>Grade Resistance (GR)</u>. Grade resistance is the resistance offered by a grade to the progress of a train. It is caused by the action of gravity, which tends to pull the train downhill. For military railway planning, use the factor of 20 pounds multiplied by the percentage of grade resistance in pounds per ton of trailing load (train).

C6.2.6. <u>Curve Resistance (CR)</u>. Curve resistance is the resistance offered by a curve to the progress of a train. No entirely satisfactory theoretical discussion of curve resistance has been published; however, engineers in the United States usually allow from 0.8 to 1 pound per ton of train per degree of curve. In military railway planning, use the factor of 0.8 pound multiplied by the degree of curvature.

C6.2.7. <u>Weather Factor (W)</u>

C6.2.7.1. The weather factor reflects, by percentage, the adverse effect of cold and wet weather on the hauling power of a locomotive. Experience and tests have proved that, whenever the outside temperature drops below 32 degrees Fahrenheit, the hauling power of a locomotive is decreased. Table C6.T3. indicates the weather factor (percent) for varying degrees of temperature.

C6.2.7.2. Ordinarily, wet weather is regarded as local and temporary; it is considered absorbed by average figures. However, in countries having extended wet seasons (monsoons, fog, etc.), the loss of tractive effort due to slippery rails may prove serious if sanding facilities are lacking or inadequate. The applicable reduction is a matter of judgement, but in general, tractive effort will not be reduced to less than 20 percent of the weight on drivers.

C6.2.8. <u>Gross Trailing Load (GTL)</u>

C6.2.8.1. When diesel-electric locomotives are operated in multiple unit operation, the gross trailing load is equal to sum of the gross trailing load for all locomotives so used. However, when the locomotives are not electrically connected for multiple-unit operation, or when steam locomotives are used in tandem (double-headed) or in pusher service, 10 percent of the total gross trailing load is deducted because of the human element involved.

C6.2.8.2. Gross trailing load is the maximum tonnage a locomotive can move under given conditions; for example, curvature, grade, and weather. It is determined by combining the factors discussed in paragraphs C6.2.3. through C6.2.7., above. The formula for gross trailing load follows:

$$GTL = \frac{DBP \times W}{RR + GR + CR}$$

where --

GTL	=	gross trailing load
DBP	=	drawbar pull
W	=	weather resistance
RR	=	rolling resistance
GR	=	grade resistance
CR	=	curve resistance

C6.2.8.3. When multiple-unit diesel locomotives or pushers are used, the gross trailing load is equal to the sum of the gross trailing load for all locomotives used.

C6.3 CHARACTERISTICS OF AND PLANNING FACTORS FOR SOME DoD LOCOMOTIVES

Table C6.T1. Characteristics of and Planning Factors for Some DoD Locomotives

Type of locomotive	Gage (inches)	Weight (pounds)	Length over couplers	Extreme width	Extreme height	Tractive force (pounds)			Horse-power	Curvature minimum radius (feet)	Fuel capacity (gallons)
						Starting at 30% adhesion	Contin-uous				
131-Ton, 0-6-6-0, domestic and foreign service, NSN-2210-554-0786	56½	262,900	55'	10'0"	14'0"	75,700	28,000 at 10 mph		1,000	231	1,600
127-Ton, 0-6-6-0, domestic and foreign service, NSN 2210-270-1354	56½	261,000	55'	10'0"	10'0"	75,700	28,000 at 10 mph		1,000	231	1,600
120-Ton, 0-6-6-0, domestic and foreign service, NSN 2210-814-5291 NSN 2210-815-3521-w/generator	56½, 60, 63, 66	240,000 246,000 w/steam generator	57'5"	9'8"	13'6"	73,000	47,000 at 10 mph		1,600	193	1,600 800 w/steam generator
120-Ton, 0-6-6-0, domestic and foreign service, NSN 2210-819-9317	56½, 60, 63, 66	240,000 246,000 w/steam generator	56'9"	9'7"	13'5"	72,000	45,000 at 10 mph		1,600	193	1,600 800 w/steam generator
120-Ton, 0-4-4-0, domestic service, NSN 2210-554-0785	56½	240,000	55'9"	10'3"	14'6"	75,000	40,000 at 11 mph		1,500	150	800
120-Ton, 0-4-4-0, domestic service, NSN 2210-262-0751	56½	246,000	48'10"	10'2"	14'6"	73,000	35,000 at 10 mph		1,200	100	750

Table C6.T1.   Characteristics of and Planning Factors for Some DoD Locomotives, continued

Type of locomotive	Gage (inches)	Weight (pounds)	Length over couplers	Extreme width	Extreme height	Tractive force (pounds)			Horse-power	Curvature minimum radius (feet)	Fuel capacity (gallons)
						Starting at 30% adhesion	Contin-uous				
115-Ton, 0-4-4-0, domestic service, NSN 2210-112-8508	56½	230,000	45'6"	10'0"	14'6"	69,000	20,000 at 15 mph		1,000	50	635
100-Ton, 0-4-4-0, domestic service, NSN 2210-819-9320	56½	199,000	44'6"	10'0"	14'4"	59,700	18,750 at 10 mph		660	50	635
100-Ton, 0-4-4-0, domestic service, NSN 2210-371-7535	56½	200,000	44'5"	10'0"	14'7"	69,700	18,750 at 10 mph		800	100	600
80-Ton, 0-4-4-0, domestic service, NSN 2210-820-5451	56½	161,000	36'10"	9'6"	13'7"	48,000	10,000 at 10 mph		500	75	400
80-Ton, 0-4-4-0, domestic service, NSN 2210-804-3614	56½	161,000	36'10"	9'6"	13'7"	48,000	10,000 at 10 mph		470	75	400
80-Ton, 0-4-4-0, domestic service, NSN 2210-804-3615	56½	161,000	41'0"	9'6"	13'4"	48,000	21,000 at 5.2 mph		550	75	400
65-Ton, 0-4-4-0, domestic service, FSN 2210-819-9319	56½	130,000	34'0"	10'1"	13'5"	39,000	9,500 at 10 mph		400	75	250

Table C6.T1.   Characteristics of and Planning Factors for Some DoD Locomotives, continued

Type of locomotive	Gage (inches)	Weight (pounds)	Length over couplers	Extreme width	Extreme height	Tractive force (pounds)			Horse-power	Curvature minimum radius (feet)	Fuel capacity (gallons)
						Starting at 30% adhesion	Contin-uous				
65-Ton, 0-4-4-0, domestic service, NSN 2210-819-9319	56½	130,000	34'0"	10'0"	13'5"	39,000	9,500 at 10 mph		400	250	
60-Ton, 0-4-4-0, domestic and foreign service, NSN 2210 819-9318	56½, 60	122,000	38'11" (Type E) 39'3" (Willison)	9'6"	13'4"	36,000	15,680 at 7.78 mph		500	75	500
45-Ton, 0-4-4-0, domestic and foreign service, NSN 2210 529-9038	56½	90,000	33'6"	9'7"	12'0"	27,000	12,000 at 6 mph		380	50	250
45-Ton, 0-4-4-0, domestic service (side rod drive) NSN 2210-821-1135	56½	90,000	28'4"	9'6"	12'0"	27,000	13,500 at 6.2 mph		300	50	165
44-Ton, 0-4-4-0, domestic service, NSN 2210-804-3610	56½	91,270	33'10"	9'4"	13'3"	26,400	11,000 at 9 mph		380	75	250
44-Ton, 0-4-4-0, domestic service NSN 2210-820-5602	56½	89,000	33'5"	10'0"	13'3"	26,400	13,000 at 7.1 mph		380	50	250
25-Ton, 0-4-0, domestic service NSN 2210-834-3202	56½	50,000	16'1"	8'7"	10'4"	15,000	6,200 at 6.2 mph		150	50	75

Table C6.T2. Average Value of Rolling Resistance

Pounds per ton of train	Condition of track
5	Exceptionally good
6	Good to fair
7	Fair to poor
8	Poor
9 and 10	Very poor

Table C6.T3. Effect of Weather on Hauling Power of Locomotives

Most adverse temperature in °F	Loss in hauling (percent)	Weather factor (percent)
Above +32	0	100
+16 to +32	5	95
0 to +15	10	90
-1 to -10	15	85
-11 to -20	20	80
-21 to -25	25	75
-26 to -30	30	70
-31 to -35	35	65
-36 to -40	40	60
-41 to -45	45	55
-46-50	50	50

Table C6.T4. Requirement for Locomotives

Type of locomotive	Type of operation	Gal. per train mile	Estimated average rate of fuel oil consumption Gal. per hour
Diesel-electric (DE) locomotive standard gauge:			
0-6-6-0, DE, 120-ton	Road switcher	2.5	11.5
0-4-4-0, DE, 120 ton	Road switcher	.9	8.0

CHAPTER 6

C7. CHAPTER 7

ACQUISITION OF LOCOMOTIVES

C7.1. STANDARDIZATION

DoD locomotive equipment provided for use in CONUS shall generally be standard, commercially designed equipment conforming to the requirements of the Association of American Railroads (AAR) and the Federal Railroad Administration (FRA). This will ensure the mobility and interchangeability of the equipment, as required. Motive power shall be of standard commercial design with types and models acquired being restricted to the minimum number consistent with current and projected requirements. Major components shall be similarly standardized to the maximum extent possible. Procurement of locomotives for foreign service shall be in accordance with the principle of acquiring commercially designed equipment, when practical, with consideration to the configuration limitations caused by clearances, axle loads, curvatures, and other restricting factors.

C7.2. PROCUREMENT CRITERIA

To avoid unnecessary military ownership, DoD-owned locomotives, to be eligible for procurement, retention, maintenance, or upgrading must meet one of the following criteria:

C7.2.1. The locomotive is a type peculiar to the military -- a specialized type not available from commercial sources, or not available in the number or at the time required to meet military needs.

C7.2.2. The locomotive is required to meet overseas or mobilization requirements.

C7.2.3. The equipment is required to meet intra-installation requirements of a military activity.

C7.2.4. The cost of obtaining locomotive service from commercial sources is in excess of the cost of operating military-owned equipment, and it can be determined administratively that it would be wasteful of public funds. This determination must comply with the provisions of DoD Instruction 4100.33, "Operation of Commercial and Industrial-Type Activities," reference (e).

C7.3. PROCUREMENT PLANNING

DoD Components having requirements for locomotive equipment not available in the DoD rail inventory or having future requirements for specialized equipment not available in the DoD or commercial railroad inventory must expeditiously requisition the equipment through appropriate channels. A minimum lead time of twenty-four months is required for procurement of specialized equipment and motive power. Prior to submitting a Military Inter-departmental Purchase Request (MIPR) the Interservice Locomotive Management Committee will be requested to determine if suitable locomotives are available within the DoD inventory that would satisfy the requirement of the DoD Component with the procurement requirement. Each DoD Component must plan, program, and budget for costs associated with the acquisition of its locomotives and locomotive equipment. TROSCOM is responsible under the DoD Coordinated Procurement Program for the acquisition of locomotives and locomotive equipment.

C8. CHAPTER 8

MAINTENANCE SUPPORT FOR LOCOMOTIVE EQUIPMENT

C8.1. RESPONSIBILITIES

C8.1.1. TROSCOM (Focal Point) is responsible for:

C8.1.1.1. Maintenance of utility rail equipment used by the Department of the Army (DA) and other DoD Agencies having Interservice Support Agreements (ISSAs) (DD Form 1144) with TROSCOM.

C8.1.1.2. Operation of Mobile Rail Repair Shops (MRRS) to provide direct and general support maintenance on this equipment. TROSCOM will ensure adequate support is available to handle other service requirements. (See section C8.6. for MRRS locations and areas they service.)

C8.1.2. Maintenance

C8.1.2.1. Unit Maintenance.

C8.1.2.1.1. The using activities are responsible for data reporting, operation, and organizational maintenance of the rail equipment.

C8.1.2.1.2. The using activities maintenance personnel, the operator, and crew of the equipment shall perform unit maintenance.

C8.1.2.1.3. On request, MRRS can perform unit maintenance for using organizations that lack the personnel, tools, or test equipment needed.

C8.1.2.2. Direct and general support maintenance. Installation commanders are responsible for direct and general support maintenance of assigned or supported equipment.

C8.1.2.3. Depot maintenance. TROSCOM is responsible for depot maintenance of Army locomotives; it shall facilitate and coordinate depot maintenance requirements of other DoD Components under the provisions of subparagraph C8.1.2.1.1., subject to the availability of shop time at depot maintenance facilities.

C8.2. REPAIR PARTS SUPPLY SUPPORT

C8.2.1. Using activities will submit requisitions to the proper MRRS for organizational maintenance repair parts not available through normal local supply channels.

C8.2.2. MRRS will:

C8.2.2.1. Verify that repair parts requisitioned are required for organizational maintenance.

C8.2.2.2. Supply items by:

C8.2.2.2.1. Shipping from MRRS stock.

C8.2.2.2.2. Making funded requisitions for parts to the proper servicing installation stock fund. (Shipment may be direct to user).

C8.2.2.2.3. Using the procurement activity of the servicing installation to obtain repair parts not available through source C8.2.2.2.1. and C8.2.2.2.2., above. (Shipment will be direct from vendors to installation.)

C8.2.2.2.4. Using Standard Form 44 (Purchase Order-Invoice-Voucher) to purchase repair parts locally in emergencies. These local purchases are subject to the limitations set out in Section 13.505-3 of the Federal Acquisition Regulation (FAR) (reference (f)).

C8.3. REPAIR PART STOCKS

C8.3.1. The MRRS are issued mission stocks and regulated items as authorized.

C8.3.2. The MRRS will replenish stocks by:

C8.3.2.1. Making funded requisitions, except items authorized for local purchase.

C8.3.2.2. Using the procurement activity of MRRS servicing installations for authorized items.

C8.4. MANDATORY INSPECTIONS

TROSCOM representatives shall conduct a mandatory annual inspection of all assigned Army locomotives. Inspections will be made for other DoD Components who request and provide funds for this service. This inspection shall be conducted regardless of the means of maintenance support and/or the organization providing the support to insure that rail equipment is maintained and reported in compliance with applicable service manuals. Locomotives that are also used on commercial track, will be maintained, inspected, and reported in compliance with the Federal Railorad Administration Regulations and the interchange rules and safety requirements of the Association of American Railroads (AAR).

C8.5. FUNDING

C8.5.1. TROSCOM provides funds for direct and general support maintenance and supply support for Class I Army installations directly to HRRS. These installations shall not cite consumer funds on requisitions.

C8.5.2. TROSCOM MRRS units provide funds for repair parts and materiel for utility rail equipment assigned to the U.S. Army Reserve Rail Shop Units.

C8.5.3. TROSCOM shall be reimbursed by customers other than Class I on Standard Form 1080 (Voucher for Transfer between Appropriations and/or Funds) for:

C8.5.3.1. Industrial Funded Installations.

C8.5.3.2. DoD Agencies covered by ISSA (DD Form 1144).

C8.5.3.3. Other Federal Agencies requesting MRRS support.

C8.5.3.4. Cost and production data shall be reported in compliance with DoD 7220.29-H (Department of Defense Depot Maintenance and Maintenance Support Cost Accounting and Production Reporting Handbook).

C8.6. SOURCE OF MAINTENANCE SUPPORT FOR LOCOMOTIVE EQUIPMENT

Mobile Rail Repair Shop (MRRS) Locations	Area Serviced
USATSARCOM MRRS #1: New Cumberland Army Deport New Cumberland, PA 17070	Connecticut, Delaware, Florida,* Georgia,* Maine, Maryland, Massachusetts, Michigan, New York, New Jersey, New Hampshire, North Carolina, Ohio, Pennsylvania, Rhode Island, South Carolina, Vermont, Virginia, West Virginia
USATSARCOM MRRS #2: Red River Army Depot Building 1535 Texarkana, TX 75501	Alabama, Arizona, Arkansas, Florida,* Georgia,* Illinois, Indiana, Iowa, Kansas, Kentucky, Louisiana, Minnesota, Missouri, Mississippi, Nebraska, North Dakota, Tennessee, Texas, Wisconsin
USATSARCOM MRRS #3: Tooele Army Depot Building 502, North End Tooele, UT 84704	Alaska, California, Colorado, Idaho, Montana, Nevada, Oregon, Utah, Washington, Wyoming

* Indicates States serviced by two MRRS:

MRRRS #1 supports Fort Stewart, GA; and Homestead Air Force Base, FL; and Cape Canaveral, FL.

MRRRS #2 supports Government Aircraft Plan #6, Marietta, GA; Marine Corps Supply Depot, Albany, GA; Moody Air Force Base, Valdosta, GA; and Warner Robins Air Force Base, GA.

C9. CHAPTER 9

REPAIR AND REPLACEMENT STANDARDS FOR LOCOMOTIVES

C9.1. GENERAL

Replacement or remanufacture of DoD locomotives shall be authorized in accordance with the provisions of this Chapter. The procedures outlined shall be used to determine the expenditure limits for locomotive repairs or eligibility for replacement.

C9.2. ONE-TIME REPAIR EXPENDITURE LIMITS

C9.2.1. Procedure

C9.2.1.1. One-time repair expenditure limits are applicable each time an item becomes unserviceable. The one-time repair expenditure limit is expressed as a percentage of the total repair cost estimate to the total cost of the end item.

C9.2.1.2. The procedure for determining the repair expenditure limit for an item follows:

C9.2.1.2.1. Establish current replacement cost.

C9.2.1.2.2. The repair cost estimate is the sum total of the estimated cost of labor and parts listed in the technical inspection repair as necessary requirements for the restoration of an end item to a serviceable condition.

C9.2.1.3. Repair eligibility shall be determined by comparing the repair cost estimate with the product of the percentage, shown on the applicable repair limitations chart, times the current replacement cost of the unserviceable end item. An end item loses its repair eligibility if the estimated cost of repair exceeds this product. The maximum allowable one-time overhaul allowance of 65 percent is restricted to those years identified in Appendix 1.

C9.2.2. <u>Expenditure Limits</u>

C9.2.2.1. The repair expenditure limit for components, assemblies, and renewable parts applicable to end items that are serviceable or are eligible for repair is 65 percent of the estimated replacement cost. New components, assemblies, and recoverable spare parts should be procured if the estimated repair cost exceeds 65 percent of the replacement cost.

C9.2.2.2. Paragraph C9.2.2.1., above, is applicable to bulk components, assemblies, and/or recoverable repair parts to be repaired and returned to the pipeline for issue. These bulk items are those items in support of the direct exchange program.

C9.2.2.3. <u>General</u>. Appendix 1 furnishes one-time repair and/or overhaul expenditure limits in percentages of price according to age of the equipment in years and provides the necessary data required to determine end item repair eligibility. All items are identified by National Stock Numbers and arranged in numerical sequence.

C9.2.2.3.1. Column (1) lists the National Stock Number (NSN) for the end item.

C9.2.2.3.2. Column (2) lists the equipment and end item nomenclature.

C9.2.2.3.3. Column (3) lists the production year of equipment for the road and serial number listed in column (4). An asterisk in this column indicates the production year is not available.

C9.2.2.3.4. Column (4) lists the road or serial number, when available.

C9.2.2.3.5. Column (5) lists the equipment age and percentage of repair expenditures allowed, in relationship to age. Lines (1) and (3) list the age of the equipment. Lines (2) and (4) list the percentages to be used to determine the repair expenditures. Lines (1) and (3) indicate the life expectancy of the item in years. Rail items to be shipped overseas or to units for movement overseas shall have a minimum of 5 years repair eligibility remaining subsequent to issue. Items to be shipped to CONUS users shall have a minimum of 1 year repair eligibility remaining subsequent to issue.

C9.3. TECHNICAL INSPECTIONS

Each locomotive shall be inspected by an experienced, technically qualified rail technican at least once annually. Unserviceable equipment shall be inspected by a qualified rail technician prior to repair or evacuation of the item to the next higher supporting maintenance facility for repair or disposal action. The inspection report shall include defects and malfunctioning components and the repair cost estimate to place the equipment in standard operating condition. The objectives of the technical inspection are:

C9.3.1. To determine the economical reparability of DoD material.

C9.3.2. To prevent the evacuation of uneconomically reparable equipment unless specifically required and directed.

C9.3.3. To preclude the loss of materiel to the Department of Defense solely on the basis of the age of the materiel.

C9.4. COMPUTATION OF REPAIR COST ESTIMATES

Before preparing detailed cost estimates review previous work orders to determine whether similar items in a similar repairable condition have been repaired. If a work order exists, use actual work order cost as the estimating basis. Old work order costs should be accelerated by using prescribed operation and maintenance inflation factors to reach an estimate of repairing the component.

C9.4.1. Cost Elements: When past experience for repairing similar components is not available to determine estimated repair costs, detailed cost computations will be necessary.

C9.4.1.1. Elements of cost to be used in estimating the cost of repair or overhaul of materiel are:

C9.4.1.1.1. Direct labor (military and civilian).

C9.4.1.1.2. Direct materiels.

C9.4.1.1.3. Indirect or overhead costs.

C9.4.1.1.4. Contractual services.

C9.4.1.1.5. Shipping and transportation costs.

C9.4.1.1.6. Other charges.

C9.4.1.2. The following elements of cost shall not be included in depot repair or overhaul unit cost estimates:

C9.4.1.2.1. Replacement of non-integral components of basic issue items.

C9.4.1.2.2. Items of operating expense; for example, replacement of batteries, antifreeze, and petroleum products, except where the replacement is required as a result of accidental damage.

C9.4.1.2.3. The labor cost of applying Modification Work Orders (MWO) except if the amount of modification labor is small so that no major materiel distortion in either modification or other depot maintenance costs will occur.

C9.4.1.2.4. The cost to overhaul or replace accessory items used to adapt materiel for special uses.

C9.4.2. Estimated Direct Labor Costs

C9.4.2.1. Direct labor is that labor, civilian or military, which can be specifically identified to the repair or overhaul job to be performed. It includes only those personnel that have direct productive contact with the materiel or service involved. Initial and final inspections are included in this category.

C9.4.2.2. To estimate direct labor costs, determine the direct labor man-hours to be applied; then, apply current pay rates, plus the cost of annual, sick and other leave and Government contributions for employee benefits.

C9.4.2.3. The determination of the direct labor man-hours to be applied shall be based on man-hour requirements for maintenance tasks listed in applicable materiel publications, commercial flat-rate manuals, when appropriate, similar work previously performed, or individual experience.

C9.4.3. Civilian Labor rates. Costs of civilian labor shall be based on the labor rate of the individuals who actually perform the maintenance service, as follows:

C9.4.3.1. Convert man-years to average productive working hours when civilian labor pay scales are stated in terms of annual salaries.

C9.4.3.2. Labor rates, whether determined from annual salaries or hourly wage rates, shall be computed to include provisions for the cost of annual, sick, and other leave, and Government-contributed fringe benefits.

C9.4.4. <u>Military Labor Rates</u>. Labor rates used for military personnel shall be the average military wage rate for the individuals performing the work based on standard rates.

C9.4.5. <u>Labor Rates, Including Indirect Expenses</u>. Heads of DoD Components, or their designees, may establish and use standard hourly rates for direct labor (including indirect or overhead). When these standard rates are established, separate rates will be established for direct support, general support, and depot for the following:

C9.4.5.1. Supportable materiel: Rail.

C9.4.5.2. Each major geographical area where wage levels vary greatly.

C9.4.6. <u>Estimate Direct Materiel Costs</u>

C9.4.6.1. Estimates of costs of all materiels directly applied and identifiable to the particular item to undergo repair or overhaul shall be included in repair and overhaul cost estimates. This includes cost of Government-furnished materiel used by a contractor in performing all or part of the maintenance jobs.

C9.4.6.2. Estimates of consumables shall be at the standard inventory price as published in appropriate supply manuals. Materiel to be obtained from local sources shall be priced at the latest invoice cost. Cost of materiel made or to be made will be the actual cost of fabrication. When actual costs are not available, engineering estimates will be used.

C9.4.6.3. Replacement parts and assemblies used in the repair process shall be at the exchange price. This is the standard inventory price less credit for the return of unserviceable reparable parts removed from the particular materiel. The applicable commodity manager may prescribe a standard credit as a percent of the standard inventory price, as long as it reflects the estimated cost to repair the returned or removed repairable part.

C9.4.7. <u>Estimated Indirect and Overhead Costs</u>

C9.4.7.1. The repair or overhaul cost estimate shall include the indirect or overhead costs associated with the repair and overhaul process. These costs shall be determined by applying the indirect or overhead rate to the estimated direct labor man-hours.

C9.4.7.2. The indirect or overhead costs used in developing the indirect or overhead rate will include:

C9.4.7.2.1. Manufacturing or production expense, such as indirect costs incurred within or identifiable to the maintenance shop or organizaton performing the repair work, although not identifiable to a particular repair or overhaul job.

C9.4.7.2.2. General and administrative expenses, such as costs incurred in general management or supervision, which are measurable costs chargeable to maintenance units and activities.

C9.4.8. Contractual Services. These are costs for contractual services required, incident to, or identifyable with the performance of all or part of the specific maintenance job and will be included in the cost estimate.

C9.4.9. Shipping Costs. All shipping costs shall be included in the estimate. Shipping costs include:

C9.4.9.1. All costs involved in preparing the materiel for shipment at point of use; and

C9.4.9.2. All transportation and handling costs from point of use to selected point of repair.

C9.4.10. Estimates of Other Costs. Any other costs, not excluded in subparagraph C9.4.1.2., required to complete the required maintenance that can be directly identified to the repair or overhaul task, shall also be included in the estimate, although not specifically mentioned herein.

C9.4.11. Commodity Manager Adjustment of Cost and Man-Hour Estimates

C9.4.11.1. When materiel is reported to a comodity manager for disposition instructions based on repair cost estimates, the comodity manager shall compare the labor rate used by field personnel with the labor rate of the depot maintenance facility selected to complete the maintenance required. Adjustments in the repair cost estimate to reflect depot maintenance labor rates shall be made prior to a decision concerning the disposition of the unserviceable asset.

C9.4.11.2. When materiel is reported to the comodity manager for disposal/instructions based on man-hour estimates, the comodity manager shall convert the direct labor man-hours and related information identifiable to the maintenance effort required to a repair or overhaul cost estimate in dollar amounts per this Regulation. This shall be done prior to a decision concerning the disposition of the materiel.

C9.4.12. <u>Waivers By Major Commands</u>

C9.4.12.1. Heads of DoD Components, or their designees, have approval authority on requests for waivers of published maximum repair and overhaul allowances when the required maintenance can be accomplished at organizational, direct support, or general support categories of maintenance. Required repairs shall not be broken into separate job estimates merely to by-pass prescribed maximum repair allowances.

C9.4.12.2. In approving such requests, commanders will insure that:

C9.4.12.2.1.. The unit or organization requesting the waiver has been unable to obtain timely replacement of the uneconomically reparable asset by checking with the appropriate comodity manager.

C9.4.12.2.2. An urgent operational or essential training requirement exists, which justifies the uneconomical repair.

C9.4.12.2.3. Resources are available (or can be made available) to the requesting organization or command to do the required repairs within an acceptable period of time. Normal maximum time is considered 60 days.

C9.4.12.2.4. Unit and activity commanders requesting materiel waivers shall submit copies of the technical inspection report with justification for materiel retention and uneconomical repair, through proper support maintenance channels, to DoD Service comanders for approval.

C9.4.13. <u>Waivers by NMP/NICP</u>. NICPs, in coordination with the proper NMP, may grant waivers to published maximum one-time repair and overhaul allowances when the maintenance required to restore the unserviceable asset to a serviceable condition will be accomplished at the depot maintenance level, and operational requirements necessitate such action.

C9.5. DISPOSITION INSTRUCTIONS

C9.5.1. Eligibility of Materiel for Evacuation to Depot Maintenance

C9.5.1.1. CONUS. All locomotives covered by this chapter are eligible for evacuation to depot maintenance whenever the Technical Inspection results indicates that repairs required are not authorized and/or exceed general support capabilities. The cost of repairs shall not exceed the one-time repair expenditure limits.

C9.5.1.2. Overseas. Depot maintenance of all locomotive end items at overseas installations is the responsibility of major overseas commanders. It shall be accomplished with existing facilities, personnel, and equipment with appropriate augmentation when required, or by contract maintenance. The technical inspectors must be familiar with maintenance operations and standards to determine the work required and thereby arrive at the proper classification.

C9.5.2. Disposition Instructions. These instructions shall be provided by the commodity manager for all locomotives regardless of repair expenditure limitations listed in the applicable appendix. When the estimated one-time repair cost exceeds the prescribed expenditure limits and waiver of limits is not authorized, no action will be taken to dispose of the equipment until disposition instructions are received from the NICP.

C10. CHAPTER 10

STORAGE OF LOCOMOTIVES

C10.1. POLICY

Locomotives authorized under the provisions of Chapter 3 may be placed in storage when there is no immediate requirement for the equipment, but it must be retained for contingency or other valid reasons. Consideration will be given to retaining the locomotive in active service through a rotation program with assigned locomotives in operation at the installation to which the unit is assigns. The high acquisition cost, the long procurement cycle the transportation costs incurred in the movement or reassignment, and the time frame required to secure a locomotive or replacement are factors to be considered in determining if a locomotive should be retained in storage or declared excess. Locomotives placed in storage shall be processed in accordance with the applicable regulations of the DoD Component owning the locomotive. The Department of the Army Technical Bulletin TB 740-93-5, "Preservation of Railroad Equipment for Storage," may be used instead of Service regulations.

C10.2. STORAGE LOCATIONS

The following factors shall be weighed in determining storage locations for locomotives:

C10.2.1. Strategic location in relation to mobilization or emergency requirements.

C10.2.2. Availability of rail trackage.

C10.2.3. Resource availability for dynamic dehumidification (cocooning) and enclosed storage facilities.

C10.2.4. Climatic conditions.

C10.2.5. Access to major trunk lines.

C10.3. STORAGE AT USER INSTALLATIONS

Administrative storage, wherein the user installation places the locomotive in a limited-care and preservation status in accordance with applicable technical manuals for short periods of time, is authorized. The allowable time that a locomotive may remain in adminstrative storage will vary with the storage environment. Locomotives placed in this type storage will be capable of being restored to full mission capability within 30 days. Prior to placing the locomotive in storage, the next scheduled preventive maintenance shall be performed and deficiencies shall be corrected. All regularly scheduled preventive maintenance services shall be suspended when the unit is placed in storage. Locomotives removed from storage will be restored to normal operating condition according to applicable technical manuals and tested to determine their operational capability.

C10.4. <u>LONG-TERM STORAGE</u>

Long-term (in excess of 5 years) storage shall be restricted to locomotives that cannot be leased or acquired in time to meet contingency requirements. Dynamic dehumidification (cocooning) should be considered when it is anticipated that the locomotives may be retained in storage in excess of 5 years. When economically and operationally feasible, locomotives should be stored in areas with climatic conditions conducive to preservation without dehumidification. Such storage will facilitate the rotation in usage of the locomotives in long-term storage and make it possible to expeditiously place locomotives in service in emergencies.

C11. CHAPTER 11

SAFETY

C11.1. OPERATING AND SAFETY RULES

Operating and Safety Rules for railroad operations will be published and kept current by the DoD Components. The Standard issued by the Association of American Railroads may be modified to apply to the conditions prevailing in the operations of the individual components. The joint Army/Air Force technical manual, TM 55-200, "Railway Operating and Safety Rules," may be used by the other DoD Components instead of preparing and maintaining individual publications. Safety rules applicable to railroad operations are incorporated into TM 55-200.

C11.2. SAFETY

The following general requirements are applicable to the operation and maintenance of all DoD locomotives.

C11.2.1. Protection Against Personal Injury. Fan openings, exposed gears and pinions, exposed moving parts of mechanisms, pipes carrying hot gases and high-voltage equipment, switches, circuit breakers, contractors, relays, grid resistors, and fuses shall be in non-hazardous locations or equipped with guards to prevent personal injury.

C11.2.2. Exhaust and Battery Gases

C11.2.2.1. Products of combustion shall be released entirely outside the cab and other compartments. Exhaust stacks shall be of sufficient height, or other means provided to prevent entry of products of combustion into the cab or other compartment under usual operating conditions.

C11.2.2.2. Battery containers shall be vented, and batteries kept from gassing excessively.

C11.2.3. General Condition. All systems and components on a locomotive shall be free of conditions that endanger the safety of the crew, working on or about locomotives or train. These conditions would include: insecure attachment of components including third-rail shoes or beams, traction motors, motor gear cases, and fuel tanks; fuels, oil, water, steam, and other leaks and accumulations of oil on electrical equipment that would create unnecessary risk; improper functioning of components, including slack adjusters, pantograph operating cylinders, circuit breakers, contractors, relays, switches, and fuses; and cracks, breaks, excessive wear and other structural infirmities of components including quill drives, axles, gears, pinions, pantograph shoes and horns, third-rail beams, traction motor gear cases, and fuel tanks.

C11.2.4. <u>Leaving Locomotive Unattended</u>. Normal circumstances should not require an engine-running locomotive to be left unattended. For unusual cases when it is necessary to leave an engine-running locomotive unattended, the following procedure should be followed:

C11.2.4.1. Securely apply locomotive hand brake.

C11.2.4.2. Place engine run and generator field switches in the OFF (down) position.

C11.2.4.3. Place throttle in IDLE and dynamic brake in OFF position. Remove reverser handle from controller to lock the controls.

C11.2.4.4. Observe all Railroad Safety precautions.

CHAPTER 11

AP1. APPENDIX 1

MAINTENANCE REPAIR EXPENDITURE LIMITATIONS FOR FSCC 2210 (LOCOMTOIVES)

NSN	Item Identification	Prod. Yr.	USA Road NR Range	Repair Expenditure Limits in Percentage of Price According to Age in Years																		
2210-00-112-8508	Locomotive, Diesel, Electric, 115 Ton, DS, ALCO Model 539S	1942 1943	7103, 7122, 7274, 7101, 7108	Yr	1	2	3	4	5	6	7	8	9	10	11	12	13	14	15	16	17	18
				%	50	49	49	49	48	48	47	47	46	46	45	44	43	42	41	40	39	38
				Yr	19	20	21	22	23	24	25	26	27	28	29	30	31	32	33	34	35	36
				%	36	35	33	32	30	28	26	24	21	18	15	10						
2210-00-142-0230	Car Spotter, DS, 8400 Lb. Draw Bar Pull, Whiting Corp.	1952 1953 1955	T-7, T-12 T-6, T-10 T-2, T-3, T-8, T-9, T-14, T-15, T-17	Yr	1	2	3	4	5	6	7	8	9	10	11	12	13	14	15	16	17	18
				%	49	49	48	46	45	44	43	41	40	38	36	34	32	30	27	24	20	12
				Yr	19	20	21	22	23	24	25	26	27	28	29	30	31	32	33	34	35	36
				%																		
2210-00-262-0751	Locomotive, Diesel, Electric, 120 Ton, DS, Fairbanks-Morse H12-44	1953	1843, 1844, 1846 thru 1853, 1855 thru 1862	Yr	1	2	3	4	5	6	7	8	9	10	11	12	13	14	15	16	17	18
				%	50	49	49	49	48	48	47	47	46	46	45	44	43	42	41	40	39	38
				Yr	19	20	21	22	23	24	25	26	27	28	29	30	31	32	33	34	35	36
				%	36	35	33	32	30	28	26	24	21	18	15	10						
2210-00-371-7535	Locomotive, Diesel, Electric, 100 Ton, DS, Electro-Motive SW-8	1951	2000, 2002, 2007 thru 2010, 2012 thru 2016, 2018 thru 2022, 2024, 2027 thru 2030, 2034 thru 2038	Yr	1	2	3	4	5	6	7	8	9	10	11	12	13	14	15	16	17	18
				%	50	49	49	49	48	48	47	47	46	46	45	44	43	42	41	40	39	38
				Yr	19	20	21	22	23	24	25	26	27	28	29	30	31	32	33	34	35	36
				%	36	35	33	32	30	28	26	24	21	18	15	10						
2210-00-529-9038	Locomotive, Diesel, Electric, 45 Ton, D&FS, GE/Caterpillar Eng.	1944	7926, 8566, 8574, 8580, 8583	Yr	1	2	3	4	5	6	7	8	9	10	11	12	13	14	15	16	17	18
				%	50	49	49	48	48	48	47	47	46	46	45	44	43	42	41	40	39	38
				Yr	19	20	21	22	23	24	25	26	27	28	29	30	31	32	33	34	35	36
				%	36	35	33	32	30	28	26	24	21	18	15	10						
2210-00-543-3289	Car Spotter, DS, 13000 Lb. Draw Bar Pull, Whiting Corp.	1956 1957	T-423 T-11, T-13	Yr	1	2	3	4	5	6	7	8	9	10	11	12	13	14	15	16	17	18
				%	49	49	48	46	45	44	43	41	40	38	36	34	32	30	27	24	20	12
				Yr	19	20	21	22	23	24	25	26	27	28	29	30	31	32	33	34	35	36
				%																		

Table header: NSN | Item Identification | Prod. Yr. | USA Road NR Range | Repair Expenditure Limits in Percentage of Price According to Age in Years

2210-00-554-0784 — Locomotive, Diesel, Electric, 25 Ton, 36" Gage, FS, GE/Cummins HBI 600 — Prod. Yr. 1943 — USA Road NR Range: 7750

	1	2	3	4	5	6	7	8	9	10	11	12	13	14	15	16	17	18
Yr	1	2	3	4	5	6	7	8	9	10	11	12	13	14	15	16	17	18
%	50	49	49	49	48	48	47	47	46	46	45	44	43	42	41	40	39	38
Yr	19	20	21	22	23	24	25	26	27	28	29	30	31	32	33	34	35	36
%	36	35	33	32	30	28	26	24	21	18	15	10						

2210-00-554-0785 — Locomotive, Diesel, Electric, 120 Ton, DS, EMD GP7L — Prod. Yr. 1951 — USA Road NR Range: 1822, 1823, 1824, 1829, 1832, 1835

	1	2	3	4	5	6	7	8	9	10	11	12	13	14	15	16	17	18
Yr	1	2	3	4	5	6	7	8	9	10	11	12	13	14	15	16	17	18
%	50	49	49	49	48	48	47	47	46	46	45	44	43	42	41	40	39	38
Yr	19	20	21	22	23	24	25	26	27	28	29	30	31	32	33	34	35	36
%	36	35	33	32	30	28	26	24	21	18	15	10						

2210-00-804-3610 — Locomotive, Diesel, Electric, 44 Ton, DS, Davenport-Besler — Prod. Yr. 1953 — USA Road NR Range: 1216, 1217, 1221 thru 1235, and 1227 thru 1231

	1	2	3	4	5	6	7	8	9	10	11	12	13	14	15	16	17	18
Yr	1	2	3	4	5	6	7	8	9	10	11	12	13	14	15	16	17	18
%	50	49	49	49	48	48	47	47	46	46	45	44	43	42	41	40	39	38
Yr	19	20	21	22	23	24	25	26	27	28	29	30	31	32	33	34	35	36
%	36	35	33	32	30	28	26	24	21	18	15	10						

2210-00-804-3611 — Locomotive, Diesel, Electric, 120 Ton, D&FS, Baldwin 606A — Prod. Yr. 1952 — USA Road NR Range: 1841, 1842, 1863, 1864

	1	2	3	4	5	6	7	8	9	10	11	12	13	14	15	16	17	18
Yr	1	2	3	4	5	6	7	8	9	10	11	12	13	14	15	16	17	18
%	50	49	49	49	48	48	47	47	46	46	45	44	43	42	41	40	39	38
Yr	19	20	21	22	23	24	25	26	27	28	29	30	31	32	33	34	35	36
%	36	35	33	32	30	28	26	24	21	18	15	10						

2210-00-804-3614 — Locomotive, Diesel, Electric, 80 Ton, DS, GE/NHBIS 600 — Prod. Yr. 1952 — USA Road NR Range: 1636, 1637, 1639 thru 1642, 1644 thru 1647, 1649, 1650, 1651, 1653 thru 1659, 1661 thru 1665, 1667 thru 1685

	1	2	3	4	5	6	7	8	9	10	11	12	13	14	15	16	17	18
Yr	1	2	3	4	5	6	7	8	9	10	11	12	13	14	15	16	17	18
%	50	49	49	49	48	48	47	47	46	46	45	44	43	42	41	40	39	38
Yr	19	20	21	22	23	24	25	26	27	28	29	30	31	32	33	34	35	36
%	36	35	33	32	30	28	26	24	21	18	15	10						

2210-00-804-3615 — Locomotive, Diesel, Electric, 80 Ton, DS, Davenport Besler — Prod. Yr. 1952 — USA Road NR Range: 1622 thru 1625, 1627, 1628, 1632 thru 1634

	1	2	3	4	5	6	7	8	9	10	11	12	13	14	15	16	17	18
Yr	1	2	3	4	5	6	7	8	9	10	11	12	13	14	15	16	17	18
%	50	49	49	49	48	48	47	47	46	46	45	44	43	42	41	40	39	38
Yr	19	20	21	22	23	24	25	26	27	28	29	30	31	32	33	34	35	36
%	36	35	33	32	30	28	26	24	21	18	15	10						

2210-00-814-5291 — Locomotive, Diesel, Electric, 120 Ton, DS, D&FS, GE/ALCO — Prod. Yr. 1953 — USA Road NR Range: 2091, 2095, 2096, 2104, 2108

	1	2	3	4	5	6	7	8	9	10	11	12	13	14	15	16	17	18
Yr	1	2	3	4	5	6	7	8	9	10	11	12	13	14	15	16	17	18
%	50	49	49	49	48	48	47	47	46	46	45	44	43	42	41	40	39	38
Yr	19	20	21	22	23	24	25	26	27	28	29	30	31	32	33	34	35	36
%	36	35	33	32	30	28	26	24	21	18	15	10						

2210-00-815-3521 — Locomotive, Diesel, Electric, 120 Ton, D&FS GE/ALCO W/Steam Generator — Prod. Yr. 1953 — USA Road NR Range: B2041 thru B2044, B2046 thru B2090

	1	2	3	4	5	6	7	8	9	10	11	12	13	14	15	16	17	18
Yr	1	2	3	4	5	6	7	8	9	10	11	12	13	14	15	16	17	18
%	50	49	49	49	48	48	47	47	46	46	45	44	43	42	41	40	39	38
Yr	19	20	21	22	23	24	25	26	27	28	29	30	31	32	33	34	35	36
%	36	35	33	32	30	28	26	24	21	18	15	10						

2210-00-819-9317 — Locomotive, Diesel, Electric, 120 Ton, D&FS, EMD-MRS-1 — Prod. Yr. 1952 — USA Road NR Range: 1808, 1809, 1810, 1812, 1813, 1820

	1	2	3	4	5	6	7	8	9	10	11	12	13	14	15	16	17	18
Yr	1	2	3	4	5	6	7	8	9	10	11	12	13	14	15	16	17	18
%	50	49	49	49	48	48	47	47	46	46	45	44	43	42	41	40	39	38
Yr	19	20	21	22	23	24	25	26	27	28	29	30	31	32	33	34	35	36
%	36	35	33	32	30	28	26	24	21	18	15	10						

2210-00-819-9318 — Locomotive, Diesel, Electric, 60 Ton, D&FS, Baldwin-Lima-Hamilton — Prod. Yr. 1954 — USA Road NR Range: 1247 thru 1273, 1275, 1276, 4001 thru 4044

	1	2	3	4	5	6	7	8	9	10	11	12	13	14	15	16	17	18
Yr	1	2	3	4	5	6	7	8	9	10	11	12	13	14	15	16	17	18
%	50	49	49	49	48	48	47	47	46	46	45	44	43	42	41	40	39	38
Yr	19	20	21	22	23	24	25	26	27	28	29	30	31	32	33	34	35	36
%	36	35	33	32	30	28	26	24	21	18	15	10						

2210-00-819-9320 — Locomotive, Diesel, Electric, 100 Ton, DS, ALCO Model 539 — Prod. Yr. 1941 / 1942 — USA Road NR Range: 1941: 7277, 7370, 7371, 7374, 7459, 7460; 1942: 1807, 7132, 7133, 7134

	1	2	3	4	5	6	7	8	9	10	11	12	13	14	15	16	17	18
Yr	1	2	3	4	5	6	7	8	9	10	11	12	13	14	15	16	17	18
%	50	49	49	49	48	48	47	47	46	46	45	44	43	42	41	40	39	38
Yr	19	20	21	22	23	24	25	26	27	28	29	30	31	32	33	34	35	36
%	36	35	33	32	30	28	26	24	21	18	15	10						

2210-00-820-5451 — Locomotive, Diesel, Electric, 80 Ton, DS, GE/Cummins LL600 — Prod. Yr. 1941 / 1942 / 1943 / 1945 / 1953 / 1954 — USA Road NR Range: 1941: 7363, 7448; 1942: 7145, 7201, 7267, 7373, 7376, 7389; 1943: 7144, 7851, 7855, 7856, 7858, 7860, 7863, 7890, 7891, 7896; 1945: 7393, 7394; 1953: 1605, 1606, 1607, 1686, 1687, 1688, 1691, 1692, 1693, 1694; 1954: 1689, 1690

	1	2	3	4	5	6	7	8	9	10	11	12	13	14	15	16	17	18
Yr	1	2	3	4	5	6	7	8	9	10	11	12	13	14	15	16	17	18
%	50	49	49	49	48	48	47	47	46	46	45	44	43	42	41	40	39	38
Yr	19	20	21	22	23	24	25	26	27	28	29	30	31	32	33	34	35	36
%	36	34	33	32	30	28	26	24	21	18	15	10						
Yr	1	2	3	4	5	6	7	8	9	10	11	12	13	14	15	16	17	18
%																		

2210-00-820-5601 — Locomotive, Diesel, Electric, 120 Ton, DS, Baldwin S/VO 8 — Prod. Yr. 1943 — USA Road NR Range: 7126, 7467

	1	2	3	4	5	6	7	8	9	10	11	12	13	14	15	16	17	18
Yr	1	2	3	4	5	6	7	8	9	10	11	12	13	14	15	16	17	18
%	50	49	49	49	48	48	47	47	46	46	45	44	43	42	41	40	39	38
Yr	19	20	21	22	23	24	25	26	27	28	29	30	31	32	33	34	35	36
%	36	35	33	32	30	28	26	24	21	18	15	10						

2210-00-820-5602 — Locomotive, Diesel, Electric, 44 Ton, DS, GE/Caterpillar D-17000 — Prod. Yr. 1942 / 1943 — USA Road NR Range: 1942: 7064, 7095; 1943: 7439, 7492, 7493, 7494, 7516, 7931

	1	2	3	4	5	6	7	8	9	10	11	12	13	14	15	16	17	18
Yr	1	2	3	4	5	6	7	8	9	10	11	12	13	14	15	16	17	18
%	50	49	49	49	48	48	47	47	46	46	45	44	43	42	41	40	39	38
Yr	19	20	21	22	23	24	25	26	27	28	29	30	31	32	33	34	35	36
%	36	35	33	32	30	28	26	24	21	18	15	10						

2210-00-821-1135 — Locomotive, Diesel, Electric, 45 Ton, DS, GE/Cummins HBI 600 — Prod. Yr. 1941 / 1942 — USA Road NR Range: 1941: 7041, 7078, 7071, 7091, 7209, 7242, 7243, 7245, 7320, 7323, 7324, 7330, 7331, 7332, 7355, 7356, 7937; 1942: 1207, 7048, 7071, 7077, 7089

	1	2	3	4	5	6	7	8	9	10	11	12	13	14	15	16	17	18
Yr	1	2	3	4	5	6	7	8	9	10	11	12	13	14	15	16	17	18
%	50	49	49	49	48	48	47	47	46	46	45	44	43	42	41	40	39	38
Yr	19	20	21	22	23	24	25	26	27	28	29	30	31	32	33	34	35	36
%	36	35	33	32	30	28	26	24	21	18	15	10						

NSN	Item Identification	Prod. Yr.	USA Road NR Range	Repair Expenditure Limits in Percentage of Price According to Age in Years																	
		1943 1944	7249, 7251, 7404, 7406, 7408, 7412, 7413, 7417, 7440, 7441, 7486, 7797, 7936 7318, 7254, 7496, 7497, 7498, 7955, 7957 8537	Yr	1	2	3	4	5	6	7	8	9	10	11	12	13	14	15	16	17	18
				%																		
				Yr	19	20	21	22	23	24	25	26	27	28	29	30	31	32	33	34	35	36
				%																		
2210-00-825-5050	Locomotive, Diesel, Mechanical, 10 Ton, DS, Plymouth Locomotive Works	1953	1032 thru 1061	Yr	1	2	3	4	5	6	7	8	9	10	11	12	13	14	15	16	17	18
				%	50	49	49	49	48	48	47	47	46	46	45	44	43	42	41	40	39	38
				Yr	19	20	21	22	23	24	25	26	27	28	29	30	31	32	33	34	35	36
				%	36	35	33	32	30	28	26	24	21	18	15	10						
2210-00-834-3202	Locomotive, Diesel, Electric, 25 Ton, DS, GE/Cummins HB 1	1943 1944 1945 1952	1136, 1182, 7098, 7763 0003, 7773, 7779 0001 1146	Yr	1	2	3	4	5	6	7	8	9	10	11	12	13	14	15	16	17	18
				%	50	49	49	49	48	48	47	47	46	46	45	44	43	42	41	40	39	38
				Yr	19	20	21	22	23	24	25	26	27	28	29	30	31	32	33	34	35	36
				%	36	35	33	32	30	28	26	24	21	18	15	10						
2210-00-837-7793	Locomotive, Diesel, Electric, 80 Ton, DS, GE/Cummins NHB!S	1952	1600 thru 1604, 1620, 1692	Yr	1	2	3	4	5	6	7	8	9	10	11	12	13	14	15	16	17	18
				%	50	49	49	49	48	48	47	47	46	46	45	44	43	42	41	40	39	38
				Yr	19	20	21	22	23	24	25	26	27	28	29	30	31	32	33	34	35	36
				%	36	35	33	32	30	28	26	24	21	18	15	10						
2210-00-939-6648	Locomotive, Diesel, Electric, 44 Ton, DS, GE/SNGLE Station, Multiple Unit	1953	1236 thru 1246	Yr	1	2	3	4	5	6	7	8	9	10	11	12	13	14	15	16	17	18
				%	50	49	49	49	48	48	47	47	46	46	45	44	43	42	41	40	39	38
				Yr	19	20	21	22	23	24	25	26	27	28	29	30	31	32	33	34	35	36
				%	36	35	33	32	30	28	26	24	21	18	15	10